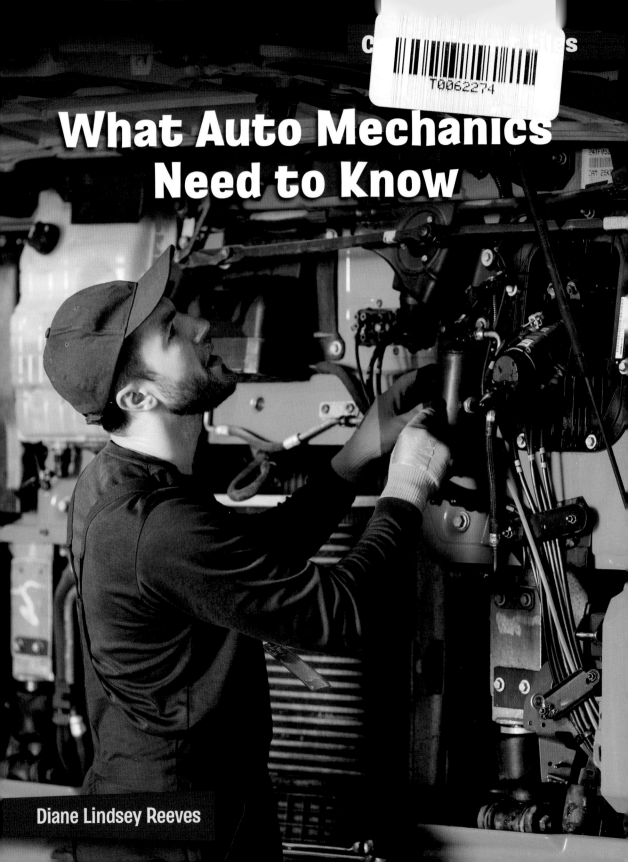

What Auto Mechanics Need to Know

Diane Lindsey Reeves

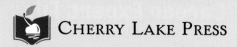

Published in the United States of America by Cherry Lake Publishing Group
Ann Arbor, Michigan
www.cherrylakepublishing.com

Reading Adviser: Beth Walker Gambro, MS, Ed., Reading Consultant, Yorkville, IL

Photo Credits: © Oleggg/Shutterstock, cover, 1; © Ground Picture/Shutterstock, 5; © Kateryna Yakovlieva/Shutterstock, 7; © Standret/Shutterstock, 8; © overcrew/Shutterstock, 9; © Sabin Coman/Shutterstock, 11; © asharkyu/Shutterstock, 13; © F8 studio/Shutterstock,14; © zkolra/Shutterstock, 15; © Svitlana Hulko/Shutterstock, 17; © Monstar Studio/ Shutterstock, 18; © LightField Studios/Shutterstock, 19; © LightField Studios/Shutterstock, 21; © Lena Makarova/ Shutterstock, 22; © Natallia Boroda/Shutterstock, 23; © Rawpixel.com/Shutterstock, 24; © riopatuca/Shutterstock, 25; © Fusionstudio/Shutterstock, 27; © Shahjehan/Shutterstock, 29

Cherry Lake Press is an imprint of Cherry Lake Publishing Group.

Library of Congress Cataloging-in-Publication Data

Names: Reeves, Diane Lindsey, 1959- author.
Title: What auto mechanics need to know / written by Diane Lindsey Reeves.
Description: Ann Arbor, Michigan : Cherry Lake Publishing, [2024] | Series: Career expert files | Includes bibliographical
    references and index. | Audience: Grades 4-6 | Summary: "Auto mechanics need to have the expert knowledge,
    skills, and tools to keep the world's automobiles running. The Career Expert Files series covers professionals who
    are experts in their fields. These career experts know things we never thought they'd need to know, but we're glad
    they do"— Provided by publisher.
Identifiers: LCCN 2023035061 | ISBN 9781668939109 (paperback) | ISBN 9781668938065 (hardcover) |
    ISBN 9781668940440 (ebook) | ISBN 9781668941799 (pdf)
Subjects: LCSH: Automobiles—Maintenance and repair—Vocational guidance—Juvenile literature. |
    Automobile mechanics—Juvenile literature.
Classification: LCC TL152 .R36 2024 | DDC 629.28/7023—dc23/eng/20230729
LC record available at https://lccn.loc.gov/2023035061

Cherry Lake Publishing Group would like to acknowledge the work of the Partnership for 21st Century Learning, a Network of Battelle for Kids. Please visit Battelle for Kids online for more information.

Printed in the United States of America

Note from publisher: Websites change regularly, and their future contents are outside of our control. Supervise children when conducting any recommended online searches for extended learning opportunities.

Diane Lindsey Reeves likes to write books that help students figure out what they want to be when they grow up. She mostly lives in Washington, D.C., but spends as much time as she can in North Carolina and South Carolina with her grandkids.

CONTENTS

In the Know

Every career you can imagine has one thing in common. It takes an expert to do them. Career experts need to know more about how to do a specific job than other people do. That's how everyone from plumbers to rocket scientists get their jobs done.

Sometimes it takes years of college study to learn what they need to know. Other times, people learn by working alongside someone who is already a career expert. No matter how they learn, it takes a career expert to do any job well.

Take auto **mechanics**, for instance. People rely on their vehicles to get to all the places they need to go. Auto mechanics keep their cars road worthy by fixing problems as well as preventing them.

Are you curious about what's under the hood of a car? Do you want to be an auto mechanic someday? Here are some things you need to know.

Top Skills for Auto Mechanics:

- **Problem-solving**
- **Communication**
- **Attention to detail**

CHAPTER 1

Auto Mechanics Know... All About Cars

Some say that the car was one of the greatest inventions in history. The alternative was to travel by horse and buggy. Cars made getting around a lot easier.

Today it is hard to imagine life without cars. People use them to get to work and run errands. They use them to explore places. People love the freedom that comes with driving a car.

Many people rely on cars for their daily transportation. This makes auto mechanics pretty important!

Mechanics need to know what each part of the car does in order to fix things.

Auto mechanics keep cars running. The career attracts people who are curious about cars. A typical mechanic can name the year, **make**, and **model** of any car. They are likely to be fascinated by how things work.

Henry Ford's Model T was the first mass-produced car. His company built and sold more than 15 million of these famous cars. Due to Ford's **assembly line** process, it only took 93 minutes to build a Model T.

In comparison, it takes 18 to 35 hours to build a modern car. This is still good time. Model Ts had about 3,000 parts. The average car now has about 30,000 parts. This explains why today's auto mechanics must be so skilled.

In many ways, modern cars have become computers on wheels. Mechanics still use tools to fix and replace parts. But they also need automotive technology skills.

CARS PAST AND PRESENT

Among the first cars sold in the United States, the Model T cost $850 in 1903. Thanks to the cost-cutting genius of Ford's assembly line, the cost fell to $260 by 1924. The average cost of a new automobile in 2023 was $48,008.

CHAPTER 2

Auto Mechanics Know... About the Systems That Make Cars Go

Cars are made up of lots of parts and pieces. Each one has a job to do. When they all work, cars operate smoothly and safely. When something goes wrong, cars break down. Auto mechanics know what all the parts of a car are supposed to do.

It all starts with a car's engine. An engine's job is to turn fuel into energy. In most cars, **internal combustion engines** use gasoline for fuel. The engine is one of the most complicated parts of a car.

An engine is the heart of a car. Car engines each have about 200 different parts on average.

There are eight major systems in gasoline-fueled cars:

- The ignition system creates an electric spark in the engine. This spark ignites a mixture of fuel and air. This happens when a driver turns the car key. When the ignition system fails, a car can stall or not start at all.

- The electrical system includes a battery, a starter, and an alternator. These parts work together to power the car. The battery makes the car's electrical current. The alternator keeps the battery charged. The starter's job is to get the engine going.

- The exhaust system has four jobs. It controls noise and keeps exhaust fumes away from passengers. It helps the engine work better. It also reduces emissions.

TRUE OR FALSE

Henry Ford invented the first gasoline-powered car.

False. Inventor credit goes to Karl Benz from Germany. Henry Ford started using the assembly line, which made it possible to mass-produce automobiles. This made it possible for more people to afford them.

Mufflers are part of the exhaust system in a car.

The shifter controls the transmission in a car, part of the drivetrain.

- Emissions include gases and other substances that cause pollution. There are three main parts of the exhaust system. They are the muffler, exhaust manifold, and catalytic converter.

- The drivetrain includes the transmission, driveshaft, axles, and wheels. Its job is to work with the engine to move the wheels.

- The suspension and steering systems work together. They allow a car to move and turn. These systems have many parts. They include the steering wheel, wheels, tires, springs, shock absorbers, and struts.

- The braking system has a big job. It must stop a car in the shortest distance possible. It includes a brake pedal, rotors, brake pads, and brake shoes.

Put all these parts together inside a frame and body and what do you get? A vehicle to take you everywhere you need to go!

MOST EXPENSIVE AUTO REPAIRS

- Engine

- Transmission

- Airbags

- Suspension

- Head gasket

CHAPTER 3

Auto Mechanics Know... How to Use the Tools of the Trade

Take a look into any auto repair shop, and one thing will be crystal clear. Auto mechanics use lots of tools. Using the right tool for the job is their number-one rule for success.

Modern cars come equipped with a computer system. This system is the Controller Area Network (CAN). It controls functions such as the transmission, brake system, and engine. That's why you'll find special computers in an auto shop. Mechanics use them to read codes from a car's computer system. This helps them figure out what is wrong.

The most obvious tools in auto shops are the lifts. These are in each of the work **bays**. These heavy-duty lifts suspend cars in the air. They allow mechanics to work under a vehicle. Using lifts properly is very important.

Lifting a car up allows mechanics to see potential problems more clearly. It's also easier to get to different parts of the car from underneath.

A socket wrench is a type of wrench auto mechanics use often.

Following safety precautions keeps people safe. In each bay, you are also likely to see a set of basic hand tools. Mechanics use these every day in their work. One of the most important tools is a set of wrenches. Wrenches come in a variety of shapes and sizes. Mechanics use them to grip, fasten, turn, tighten, and loosen nuts and bolts.

There are other basic tools in a mechanic's tool kit. These include screwdrivers, pliers, hammers, and rachets and socket sets. There are many ways these small tools help get big jobs done.

Mechanics in auto shops also share many other tools. They use car jacks to raise cars off the ground to change tires. Air compressors inflate tires and blow dirt out of hard-to-reach places under the hood.

They also use battery chargers and jumpers to recharge car batteries. They use engine hoists to lift heavy engines. They use brake lathes to resurface brake rotors and drums.

If there is a common problem in auto repair, there is a tool to fix it. It's a hands-on job, and mechanics learn to use them all.

YOUR TURN

With an adult, find pictures online of the following tools: screwdriver, wrench, torque wrench, pliers, ratchet and socket set, vehicle jack, and multimeter. Make a chart showing the tools. Include a brief description of what each one is used for.

CHAPTER 4

Auto Mechanics Know... How to Keep Cars Safe for the Road

There is no doubt about it. Cars are amazing machines. But they can also be dangerous. Mechanics do everything they can to make cars safe. Some states require cars to be inspected by a mechanic every year. Mechanics make sure cars are safe in three main ways.

Passenger safety is a high priority. Cars are inspected. Mechanics make sure that seat belts and door locks are working. If an airbag warning light is on, they recommend having it fixed right away. Keeping these safety features in good repair protects passengers.

Mechanics do safety checks in cars to ensure drivers are safe on the road. Functional seat belts, airbags, and locks all keep people safer.

Windshield wipers need to be replaced about every 6 months to a year.

Mechanics also look for ways to keep vehicles—yours and others—safe. They make sure all lights and turn signals work. This makes it easier for drivers to see and be seen. They also make sure that windshield wipers work. It is dangerous to drive in rain or snow without them.

The environment is another thing mechanics want to keep safe. They do this by monitoring the car's emissions. A mechanic may need to fix a car's exhaust system. They also make sure tires are inflated to the right pressure. Well-inflated tires use less gasoline. This results in less pollution.

SAFETY COUNTS

New advanced car safety features really work. Research shows they reduce the risk of serious crashes. They also lower injury risks. These features include **blind-spot monitoring** and **lane-keeping assist**. **Collision** warning systems and automatic emergency brakes are others.

Electric cars now are so common that there are charging stations in many parking areas.

Learning to work on electric cars and other hybrids is becoming more important. Cars like the Toyota Prius use special batteries. These types of cars are becoming more popular. So are those that use alternative fuels. Auto mechanics will need to know how to fix them.

INSPECTOR ON DUTY

Ask a parent to help you inspect your family's car. Check to make sure the lights, turn signals, and windshield wipers work. See that all seat belts click safely into place. Are there any cracks in the windshield or windows? Is smoke coming out of the muffler? Any problems you spot should be fixed as soon as possible.

CHAPTER 5

Auto Mechanics Know... How to Find the Job They Want

Modern vehicles are complicated. It is impossible for one person to know everything about each one. That is why you find different kinds of auto repair shops. They include tire stores, body shops, and oil and lube service centers. Some repair shops work with certain brands of cars. Others work on motorcycles or boats.

All this variety is also why mechanics often specialize in certain types of auto repair. Some of these specialties:

Auto body mechanics repair vehicles that have been damaged. These vehicles were likely in collisions or accidents. They repair or replace bumpers, headlights, doors, and panels. Their work can also include painting and other finishing touches.

Different tools are needed for auto body work. Special sanders and paint sprayers are often used by auto body mechanics.

Auto glass mechanics remove, repair, and install glass. They install windows and windshields. Some work in shops. Others do the repairs at a client's home or business.

Brake and transmission technicians work on braking and steering systems. They also fix transmission power trains.

Diesel mechanics work on vehicles that have diesel engines. These include fire trucks and ambulances. They also include construction vehicles like bulldozers and cranes. Diesel engines are more expensive, so they are only used in some U.S. automobiles.

MORE CAREERS WITH CARS

Some auto careers need people who design. Designers create how cars look. Some auto careers need engineers. They engineer how all the automobiles' parts work. New high-tech opportunities are emerging for designers and engineers. They can create self-driving and environmentally friendly cars.

Every second it takes to change tires and make repairs in the pit is a second lost out on the racetrack. Race car mechanics have to be fast at their jobs!

General mechanics work on different types of cars, trucks, and automobiles. They tend to be more experienced. They know a lot about vehicle mechanical and electrical systems.

Race car mechanics work as part of the skilled pit stop crews during races. They also get race cars into tip-top shape before and after races.

Service technicians help prevent problems before they happen. They use diagnostic tools to check systems in a car. They change oil and filters and run emissions tests.

Activity

Stop, Think, and Write

Can you imagine a world without cars? What if people could only go as far as their feet could take them?

Get a separate sheet of paper. On one side, answer these questions:

- *How do auto mechanics make the world a better place?*
- *Are you curious about cars?*
- *Do you like fixing things and working with tools?*
- *Can you imagine yourself being an auto mechanic someday?*

On the other side of the paper:

- *Draw a picture of you repairing your favorite type of vehicle.*

Things to Do If You Want to Be an Auto Mechanic

Any car owner will tell you that a good mechanic is worth their weight in gold. Here are some things you can do to get ready to be an auto mechanic someday.

NOW

- Help your parent or another trusted adult with minor car repairs at home.

- Learn all you can about the makes, models, and special features of cars.

- With a trusted adult, search the Internet to find out more about how engines work. Read up on other interesting facts about cars and their care.

LATER

- Take a basic auto mechanic course at a trade school. Some programs offer training to work on specific brands of cars.

- Consider earning an associate of applied science (AAS) degree in auto technology or auto repair.

- Earn an Automotive Service Excellence (ASE) certification by passing tests.

Learn More

Books

Bova, Dan. *Road and Track Crew's Big and Fast Cars.* New York, NY: Hearst Home Kids, 2022.

Gitlin, Martin. *Careers in Self-Driving Car Technology.* Ann Arbor, MI: Cherry Lake Publishing, 2019.

Ralphs, Matt. *Transported: 50 Vehicles that Changed the World.* Lincoln, MA: Nosy Crow, 2023.

Reis, Ronald A. *Henry Ford for Kids: His Life and Ideas.* Chicago, IL: Chicago Review Press, 2016.

On the Web

With an adult, learn more online with these suggested searches.

Car and Driver — How a Car Is Made: Every Step from Invention to Launch

How Stuff Works — How Cars Work

Society of Automotive Historians website

Glossary

assembly line (uh-SEM-blee LIYN) a way to build a product by breaking it into a step-by-step process that is repeated task after task along a line of workers

bays (BAYZ) partly enclosed areas inside an auto repair shop that are used by mechanics to work on a specific vehicle

blind-spot monitoring (BLIEND-SPAHT MAH-nuh-tuhr-ing) a warning system that detects vehicles traveling in areas that cannot be seen in sideview or rearview mirrors

collision (kuh-LIH-juhn) a crash between moving things or people

emissions (ee-MIH-shuhnz) greenhouse gases and pollutants released by a car

internal combustion engines (in-TUHR-nuhl kuhm-BUHS-chuhn EN-juhnz) engines that burn fuel inside to create energy

lane-keeping assist (LAYN-KEE-ping uh-SIST) systems designed to provide steering support to prevent drivers from veering into another lane

make (MAYK) the name of the company that manufactures a specific car, such as Chevrolet or Honda

mechanics (mih-KAH-niks) people who repair and maintain machines such as automobiles

model (MAH-duhl) a specific product manufactured by a car company

Index